Buffy the vampire slayer

CHAOS BLEEDS

REUNION

Buffy
the vampire slayer™

Pedigree®

Published by Pedigree Books Limited
Beech Hill House, Walnut Gardens,
Exeter, Devon, EX4 4DH.
E-mail books@pedigreegroup.co.uk

Published 2004

£6.99

CHARACTERS

Buffy

Buffy Summers was just your average pom-pom shaking prom queen when she found out that she was the latest in a line of 'chosen ones' - a vampire slayer. After she torched the school gym in her first major fight with the vamps, her mother moved her to Sunnydale, California, to start a new life. But Buffy's work had only just begun - Sunnydale, was built on top of a Hellmouth, complete with vampires, demons and other assorted evils. Buffy has gone through death, resurrection, the loss of her true love and the death of her mother, not to mention the stress of watching her best friend almost destroy the world. But with her super-strength and quick intelligence, not to mention her loyal Scooby Gang, she's more than a match for any big bad that comes her way!

Giles

Rupert Giles is Buffy's watcher - a book loving Oxford graduate who became a librarian at Sunnydale High in order to train and guide Buffy. Giles was a father figure to the young slayer, providing strong emotional support alongside weapons training. After Buffy left highschool Giles bought the Magic Box Shop, since Giles has moved back to England he has left the Magic Box in Anya's hands.

Spike

An arrogant bloodthursty and witty vampire from 19th century England, Spike first arrived in Sunnydale determined to make Buffy the third slayer he'd killed. But after a chip was implanted in his head to make him harmless to humans, Spike began to work on the side of the slayer. His sharp tongue and street attitude still get him into trouble on a pretty regular basis but the Scooby Gang is slowly learning to trust him. Spike's relationship with Buffy continues to grow as they become closer and closer.

Tara

Tara Maclay, a talented witch, she met Willow at university and soon became a valuable member of the Scooby Gang. Tara is gentle and kind, with an inner strength which makes her a loyal friend and a trustworthy confidant. Unfortunately her untimely death has caused the dark magic within Willow to be released.

CHARACTERS

Willow

When Buffy arrived at Sunnydale High Willow Rosenberg was a shy quiet girl who's intelligence and computer wizardry soon made her invaluable to the slayer. Buffys best friend, Willow became interested in magic and grew to be a very powerful witch. Although she was addicted to dark magic for a while, the friendship of the Scooby Gang pulled her through. She gives Buffy the emotional and magical support she needs.

Xander

Unlike Willow and Buffy Xander Harris has no special powers, but his role in the Scooby Gang is just as vital. With his jokes and wisecracks, Xander raises everyone's spirits. His friendship and loyalty never waiver, and what he lacks in supernatural powers he more than makes up for in heart.

Anya

Anyanka, Patron Saint of Scorned Women, is a vengeance demon who has so far been alive for 1,124 years. She first came to Sunnydale to wreak havoc on behalf of angry women, but when Giles destroyed her amulet she lost her powers and became an ordinary student at Sunnydale High. With her unexpected kindness and her blunt honesty, Anya is an integral member of the Scooby Gang, once again Anya has become a vengeance demon.

Dawn

Buffys little sister, Dawn, appeared out of nowhere one day - and for a while no one realised she had'nt always been there! Eventually the Scooby Gang figured out that she was really the Key - a powerful energy source that could be used to open hell on earth. Dawn has learnt to fight side by side with the rest of the scooby gang. Like Xander, she sometimes finds it hard to be without supernatural powers, but her love for her sister and her friends always gives her strength.

Buffy
the vampire slayer™

Pinup 1

Pinup 2

THAT'S WHAT HAPPENS, HONEY. STORY OF MY LIFE. THE BOYS GET A TASTE OF SARA, THEY CAN'T HELP COMIN' BACK FOR MORE.

I CAN SEE WHY.

ONLY THIS TIME, *I'M* GONNA BE THE ONE DOIN' THE THRUSTING.

I'M GONNA SCRATCH YOU, MISTER. GONNA RIP YOU RIGHT OPEN WITH MY PRETTY LADY FINGERS.

THIS IS JUST *WRONG.*

STAND STILL, GIRL. WE'RE JUST ABOUT FINISHED HERE.

LEST THE BARRIER BE SUNDERED, LEST THE BARRIER FALL. SEAL THE BREACH. CLOSE THE DOOR.

29

Willow

Buffy
the vampire slayer™

Buffy
the vampire slayer™

Reunion

...IT COMES.

UNHHH!

ZSSSSS

KKKKRR

KK

RWWW

"XANDER? WHAT ARE YOU TRYING TO INDICATE WITH THAT UNEXPLAINED SOUND? SOME KIND OF CREAKING?"

DON'T HURT BUFFY! PLEASE!

"THAT COULD KILL IT? A FALLING ∠? I DON'T BUY IT."

"IT'S DUMB."

WHAT?

SORRY, BUT HE DIDN'T CALL HER TO PUT HER IN DANGER. HE WOULDN'T DO THAT. HE CALLED HER BECAUSE IF HE DIDN'T SEE HER, HE WOULD DIE.

ACTUALLY, HE'S ALREADY DEAD.

YOU KNOW WHAT I MEAN. I MEAN HIS HEART SPOKE OF HER WITH EVERY TORTURED BEAT.

ACTUALLY, HIS HEART DOESN'T BEAT.

OKAY, YOU HAVE TO STOP WITH THE *ACTUALLIES*...

OH, ANGEL.

BUFFY.

"IS SOMETHING ADVENTUROUS GOING TO HAPPEN SOON?"

"WHAT'S THAT ON THE BEACH OVER THERE? A CAMPFIRE?"

45

"SO THEY'RE AT THE DENNY'S IN OXNARD--"

"HEY! ANYA! I THOUGHT YOU WEREN'T GOING TO TELL THIS!"

"I'M *NOT*! I MEAN, I AM, BUT I CAN'T *HELP* IT! IN MY STORY, THIS IS WHERE BUFFY AND ANGEL CHOSE TO MEET..."

"THEY'VE DECIDED THAT THEY NEED TO BE SOMEPLACE WHERE THEY CAN REALLY *TALK*."

I'M GLAD WE CAME SOMEPLACE WHERE WE CAN REALLY *TALK*.

ALSO, THIS BURGER IS ESPECIALLY JUICY.

YES, WE NEED THIS MUCH MORE THAN WE NEED VIGOROUS SEXUAL INTER-COURSE.

YOU LOOK GOOD. YOU LOOK THE SAME... WHICH IS GOOD.

NOT TO ME. I LOOK IN THE MIRROR AND SOMETIMES I HAVE NO IDEA WHO THAT IS IN THERE.

THAT'LL PASS. YOU'LL FIND YOURSELF PULLED BACK INTO THE WORLD.

I DON'T KNOW.

TRUST ME. I'VE BEEN WHERE YOU ARE.

"OH... *THAT'S* NOT THE FIRE DEMON."

"NOPE. THIS IS THE DEMON I INTENDED TO TELL ABOUT. *SCARY,* HUH? GUESS I'M IN CONTROL OF THIS STORY AFTER ALL!"

"THEY HAVE *VERY* STRONG LEGS. *TERRIFYING.*"

"I DON'T REMEMBER IT HAVING THOSE KINDS OF HANDS AND FEET..."

GRROO

WHAT-- WHAT'S HAPPENING TO YOU?

KRRRRRRRR

"IT'S HIM."

SSSSSSZ

ANGEL! WAKE UP! I NEED HELP!

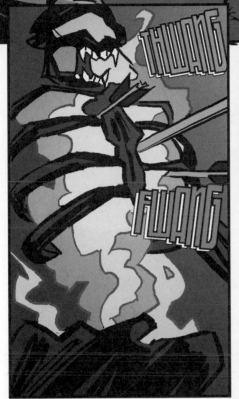THWANG

FWANG

NO! THE BOOKS!

HE'S GOING TO BURN THE STORE DOWN AROUND US!

UM... THAT'S AN EXPENSIVE ANCIENT SHROUD...

AND YOU THOUGHT SHE WASN'T NORMAL. SHE DEFEATED THAT GUY PRETTY FAST!

OH NO! HE'S ALL...HE'S UP!

FWOOSH

URRRGHH!

So, Dawn, why are you telling all these stories about me and Angel?

Um... is *that* what we said we were doing?

Willow?

Willow? The ingredient you went to buy... what spell did you do, any-way?

"NOTHING."

Compel her, O spirit. Buffy holds a secret in her heart. Make her speak of her encounter with the vampire called Angel. Open her up, let us see. *COMPEL.*

I will find her. I will open her. I will bring you her heart.

No! NOOO! THAT'S NOT WHAT I MEANT!

Doesn't really matter, any-way. It all turned out okay!

THE END

61